CATCH OF THE DAY

Put the fishing lines in order from short to long. The shortest line gets number 1, the longest one gets number 5.
Draw a circle around the biggest fish.

to ma... and to ...derstand the concept of length

IN A ROW

Look carefully at these sequences of shapes and colors. Complete the pattern in each row.

PRETTY NECKLACE

Coco Crocodile has made a beautiful necklace. Count the different kinds of beads, looking carefully at their shape and color, then fill in the table below.

GOAL:
to read a table and to think logically

	Red	Yellow	Blue
● Circle			
♥ Heart			
✱ Flower			

MMMARVELOUS

Which of these objects have
the letter M in them?
Color them in.

GOAL:
to recognize letters

M

CRAWLING CRITTERS

Some of these creatures are insects, others aren't. Only color in the insects.

GOAL:
to classify objects

AYE, AYE, CAPTAIN!
Connect the sea captains with their boats.
Tip: the letters on their shirts
might give you a clue.

GOAL:
to recognize letters

SPACE TRAVEL

Let's go and explore space!
Trace over the dotted lines
to finish the spacecrafts.

GOAL:
to develop
manual dexterity

SNAPSHOTS
Ask a grown-up to read the sentence below each picture. Listen carefully: there's something wrong. What is it?

GOAL:
to practice listening comprehension

Sarah is twirling her jump rope.

There is not much traffic on the road today.

The farmer is knitting a nice scarf.

The diver has found a box full of gold.

STRANGE FISH

These funny looking fish look a lot like the shapes on the right. Color each fish in the same color as the similar shape.

GOAL: to recognize shapes and colors

EGG-CELLENT!

These boxes can hold 10 eggs. How many eggs are under the cloth in each box? Write the number in the circle.

GOAL:
to add up to 10

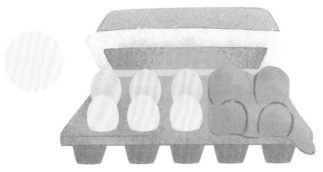

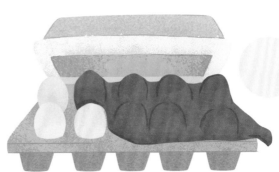

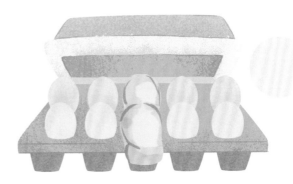

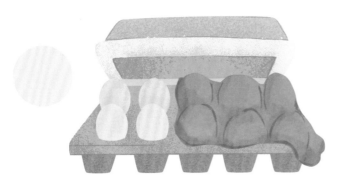

AT THE AIRPORT

There are lots of letters and numbers at the airport. Color the objects showing numbers in red and the ones showing letters in blue.

GOAL:
to recognize letters and numbers

PASSPORT CONTROL

582

46

5179

NEW YORK

PARIS

123

LUGGAGE

ALL ABOARD!
Each railroad car has a letter on it.
If you can trace over the dotted lines,
you can write letters!

BUSY BUILDER

Look at the blocks that form the building at the top. Which of the three sets of blocks below could make the same building?

GOAL: to recognize similarities and differences

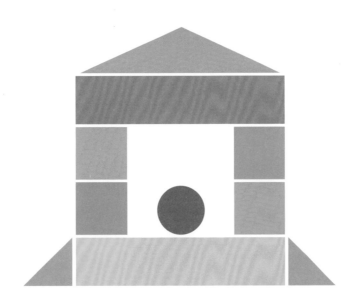

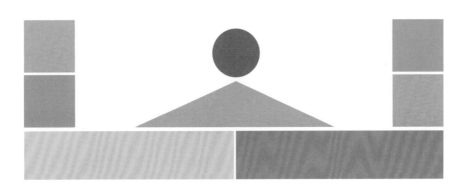

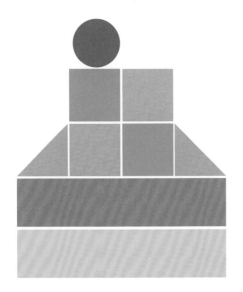

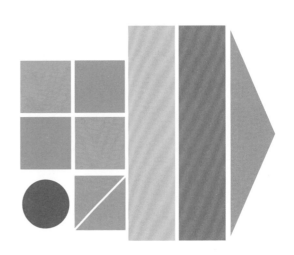

ONE LESS

Copy the pictures on the left into the boxes on the right, making sure that your drawings always contain one less shape than in the original.

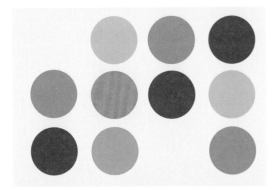

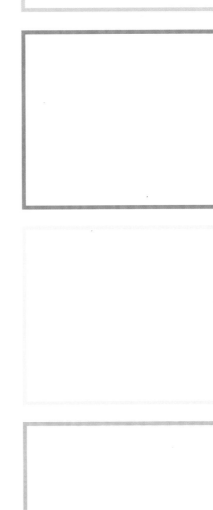

THE RIGHT TOOLS FOR THE JOB

Connect each character on the left
with the thing they need to do their job.

BLUB BLUB

Count the bubbles produced by each fish
and color them in to match the fish.
Color the matching number
in the same color.

GOAL:
to count to 17 and
to recognize numbers

5

6

10

12

17

FROSTY WINTER

In each row, draw a circle around the group with the fewest objects.

GOAL:
to count and to understand the concept of "fewest"

COLORFUL UNIVERSE

Complete this table. In each row, draw the same space object as on the left. The colors at the top show you what color to make each object.

FIELDS OF FLOWERS

Solve the addition problems on the left.
Count the flowers on the right. Connect each
sum with the matching flower group.

GOAL:
to solve sums
up to 10

6+1= ▢ •   •

4+3= ▢ •   •

3+1= ▢ •   •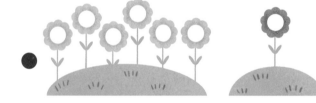

4+2= ▢ •   •

4+4= ▢ •   •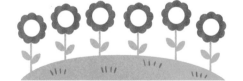

4+6= ▢ •   •

FLUTTERING FRIENDS
Copy the dotted butterfly onto the empty board. Be careful to give every dot the right color.

GOAL:
to develop spatial awareness

MATCHMAKING

Can you make pairs from the illustrations below? Draw a line between the two linked objects.

GOAL: to make associations

FILL IN THE GAPS

Study each row of fruit. There is always one fruit missing. Find it in the box below and draw a line to put it in the right place.

GOAL: to complete sequences

A FAIR SHARE

Connect each birthday cake on the left
to its missing slice on the right.

GOAL:
to develop
spatial awareness

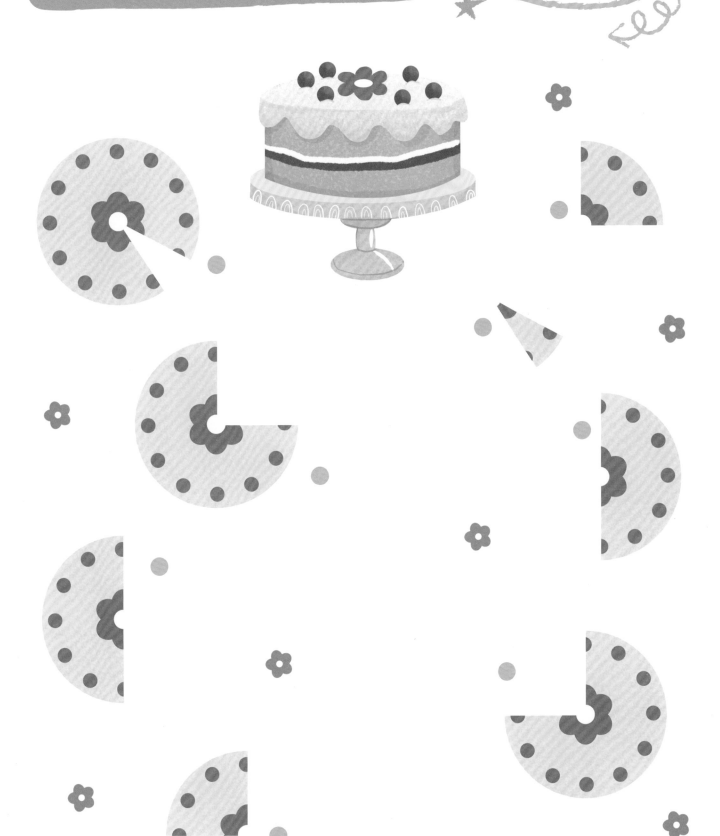

BEEP BOOP

Each robot has a number on its belly.
If you can trace over the dotted lines, you
can write the numbers from 1 to 10!

GOAL: to develop manual dexterity and to write numbers

FAIRY HOUSES

Each fairy lives in a mushroom
with a different number of spots.
Draw in the missing spots so that
each mushroom has the number shown.

GOAL:
to count to 15

HAPPY AND SAD
Look for pairs of opposites.
Connect each illustration on the left
with its opposite on the right.

GOAL:
to make comparisons
and to understand the
concept of opposites

MUSIC MAESTRO!
Connect each virtuoso with the correct picture. Which musician does not have a picture? Cross this animal out.

TELL ME A STORY
Ask a grown-up to read the sentence below each picture. Listen carefully: there's something wrong. What is it?

GOAL:
to practice listening comprehension

Bruno Bear is enjoying the nice summer day.

Henry Hamster loves splashing water on Ellie Elephant.

Clive Crocodile is an expert with his guitar.

Dotty Dino is leading the race.

UNDER CONSTRUCTION

In which order was this house built?
Put these drawings in the right order.
The first step gets number 1,
the last one gets number 6.

GOAL:
to think logically

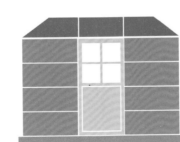

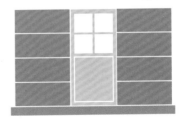

BLUE PLANET

Count each group of underwater creatures
and write the number in the box.

GOAL:
to count to 19

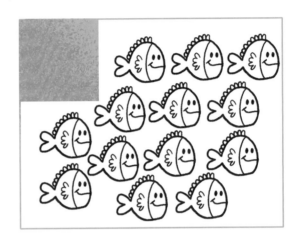

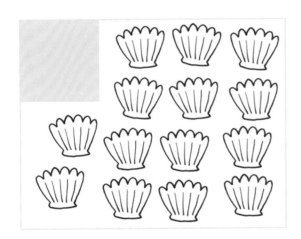

SWEET DREAMS

Ollie Owl is having a beautiful dream.
Find your way through the maze to
discover what he is dreaming about.

GOAL:
to develop
manual dexterity

HOME LIBRARY

Which books have the same letters on them?
Color these in the same color.

CLAP AND COLOR

Say these words out loud. Clap out
the parts of the word as you say them.
How many are there?
Color in that number of circles.

GOAL:
to stimulate
auditory perception

IN PERFECT SHAPE

Each box should have 6 different shapes.
Which one is missing in each box?
Draw a line from the shape
at the bottom to the right box.

BLOWING BUBBLES

Solve the addition problems and connect them with the right answer. If you need help, you can count the bubbles.

⬤ + ⬤ = ...   **9**

⬤⬤ / ⬤⬤ + ⬤⬤ / ⬤ = ...   **5**

⬤⬤ / ⬤ + ⬤⬤ / ⬤⬤ = ...   **2**

⬤⬤ / ⬤⬤ + ⬤⬤ / ⬤⬤ ⬤ = ...   **7**

⬤ / ⬤ + ⬤⬤ / ⬤ = ...   **6**

CRAFTY BIRDHOUSE

Put these scenes in the right order.
What happens first gets number 1,
what happens last gets number 6.

GOAL:
to think logically

BIRDHOUSE

BUILDING BLOCKS

How many blocks are used to build
each of these constructions?
Write the number in each box.

GOAL:
to develop
spatial awareness

MASTER ARTIST

Trace over the dotted lines to
finish the drawings and words.
Congratulations!
You can write words!

GOAL:
to develop
manual dexterity

CLOUD

SUN

BEE

BEAR

WHAT'S IT MADE OF?
Which object is made of which material?
Connect each object to the right material.

GOAL:
to make associations

MILK

FIRE ENGINE

Help Brady Bear get to his fire engine.
He can only get there by stepping
on the triangles.

GOAL:
to recognize shapes

LION OVERBOARD!
Help Louie Lion swim back to his boat.
Follow the letters in the right order:
A B C D E F G H

GOAL:
to recognize letters and
to learn the alphabet

IN THE DARK
Find the right shadow
for each fuzzy monster.

GOAL:
to recognize
similarities and
differences

LIKE DAY AND NIGHT

Find the pairs of opposites.
Draw lines to connect each pair.

YUM, DINNERTIME!
Follow the wires and find out what
each friend is having for dinner.

GOAL:
to develop
manual dexterity

PICTURE PERFECT

Ask a grown-up to read the sentence next to each picture. Listen carefully: there's something wrong. What is it?

GOAL: to practice listening comprehension

Clara built the tallest tower.

Ruby has 6 puppies.

John is enjoying an ice cream.

Bunny is sad in the winter.

BAMBOO BRUNCH
Connect each panda group with the right bamboo group so that every panda can enjoy one delicious twig.

GOAL:
to count to 8

ODD ONE OUT

In each group, color in everything
that is related to the colored object.

What is the odd one out?

BEYOND THE STARS

Spell out the word PLANET by drawing
a circle around the right letters.

GOAL:
to recognize letters

L
S

R
E

O
A

P
Y

N

T
K